Mirrored Reflections

Connie Berger

BookLeaf
Publishing

India | USA | UK

Presentation by *BookLeaf Publishing*

Web: www.bookleafpub.com

E-mail: info@bookleafpub.com

ISBN: 9789358369984

First edition 2023

I dedicate my work to God without his strength I wouldn't be here. My best friend; the man I love for loving me enough to inspire me to be better. To my daughter for always being there to reminding me to never give up and to my mom for being my strong source of faith that I have.

ACKNOWLEDGEMENT

I would like to first thank God, those my heart has loved, my family, and my friends who have brought the pages to life.

PREFACE

For more than 15 years I have been trying to establish a career in writing song lyrics unsuccessfully. I have more than 22 writings or works in progress. Most of my time is spent trying to think of creative titles for songs or catch lines that will attract the attention of those who read my work. I have had a few muses during my journey that sparked my progress when I would find myself stuck.

Do You Believe?

Do you believe in fate?
Do you believe in ...
Finding that one heartfelt soul mate?
Do you believe ...
No matter how late in life;
Destiny will achieve
Bringing you a husband
Or wife,
To accompany you ...
To see you through it all?
Truly it's your call...

We're each given
A God-given choice...
A divine inspiration
To rejoice in;

Reflect upon...
And meditate,
Before it's too late...

Do you believe in fate?
Do you believe in it?
Finding that one heartfelt soul mate?
Do you believe,
Love opens up doors.

To believe,
First, you have to receive...
Open your heart;
Trust for a new start...
Forever maybe ;
Too late to wait...
Would it be your mistake...?
Your biggest regret,
To ever forget?

Do you believe in it?
Finding that one heartfelt soul mate?
Do you believe ...
In happy ever after?

Don't be deceived;
By decisions
To keep deciding...
If you're finally ready,

To give your thoughts
Rest and just...
Live life,
Without regrets.

Have you came
To a conclusion yet?
Do you believe in it?
Finding that one heartfelt soul mate?
Do you believe ...?

Blessed Regrets

Blessed Regrets

With tear-filled eyes
I watched my
Destiny walk away
With one last goodbye;
I knew he had to be you~
Without a word ...
I cried wondering why
Life tried to barren
The womb ;
Making me feel unworthy
to conceive your love

Everything I ever wanted
I found in your company...

Somebody
was to accompany you...
Through journey around...
Trusting that God's plans
Were uncomfortable,
But better for you,
I lived a lie
Of pretending,
I didn't love you...
Didn't want to.
Pretending I didn't
Want you...
Trying to
Cover up
All the pain
That rained down regrets.

Functioning day by day
Was abundantly clear
Watching your movements;
Witnessing your improvements;
Reluctantly I could see
There was another part of you...
About to be free...
It didn't take a master's degree
To see all that all of my regrets
We're your blessing
To my life lessons.

Another Place, Another Time

There's a perfect space,
Someplace in my mind,
Where I find
Another place
Another time
I wanna return to it.
A time when dreams
Don't have demons,
Your world becomes mine
Stars don't forget to shine
The hands of time rewind...
A place that's captured my heart,
Defies this Destiny of ours
Pretending it's just
You and me...
Seeing our way through

Those uncomfortable emotions
That mask...
Things that don't always last.

There's a perfect space
Some place in my mind
Where I find
Another place,
Another time.
That reminds me...
Of rainbows
Sunshine,
And all that's divine
The promises of my desires
And all it requires
To provide you
with unconditional love,
That has been written
From above
From my heart...
To yours from
That first date...
In Another place,
Another time...

It's a Little TOO Late

A Little to Late..

It's a little too late...
To save whats,
Not within the;
Hands of fate...

A little bit too late...
To set things straight...
It's way too late...
To live with no regrets...
Forgetting the mess...
Created from a past test
In the hands of faith...
...
It's a little too late,
To start over new...
Pretending that things...
Would just fall into place...

OOoh if we only knew
What life would bring...
Us through,
Couldnt be bound by glue...

Couldn't be bound by ties that;
Bind those memories.

Would we be ready too?
Embrace the chance...
To erase the past...
Everyplace,
In time and space;
Faced face to face...
Someplace,
Interlaced with traces
Of fond reminiscences...

It's a bit too late...
To replace
What you've done did.
There no way to
Rebuild, reconstruct,
A resurrection
Of destruction...
No way to bring back time;
It's already been fulfilled.
Tic toc
Times stood still

Ghost of Christmas Past

Hanging displayed for all to see
My Ghost of Christmas Past
Decorated nicely by this heart within me
Unconditional love dropping
Like Tinsel shining through
Every branch of this destiny of mine
My tears spilled down covering
Like decorations on a tree...
My feelings lay open
And exposed,
Baring all my stupidity
And nativity
Believing in things not meant to be
With just one wish
That'd shine like
The star in your eyes,

Instead, you sit on a memory
The Ghost of a Christmas Past
Your reflection shimmers through,
 Like twinkling little multi-colored lights
smiling back at me ... year after year
Always there,
Reminding me
It takes two

To truly connect
In the future,
That of a ghost
of Christmas past
To make something last...
I'll leave this one last,
For the one whose birthday it rest.

Through the Window of Blind Eyes

Through the Windows of Blind Eyes

Through the Window of Blind Eyes
I saw the love,
Felt the pain
Walked a thin line
And shouldered a lot of blame...

I tried to hide my pride,
Pushed away the tears
I cried,
That threatened

All my worst fears...
Mirrored back at me...
Through the many years,
I spent protecting
The reflection of,
what I did not
Want to clearly see...

Through the Window of Blind Eyes
I hid...
Behind
The projection of lies,
Holding onto a hope,
That lost its place
Through space and time...

I believed in second chances
Refusing to see the circumstances...
Reliving in a fairytale romance
Held within my head...
Taking advances to
Cradle the love I felt in my heart,
Trying to rekindle that spark
That got left somewhere
Within the dark...
But...,
An act of God
Stepped in
Ripped this picture,

I had painted
Spinning my world apart...
Taking control
Over this facade...

Through the Window of Blind Eyes
I hid...
Behind
The projection of lies,
Holding onto a hope,
That lost its place
Through space and time...

I created my own story...
An art of fiction,
Set with boundaries
Self addictions
And the mess of restrictions
That couldn't be overcome...
On my own...

Through the Window of Blind Eyes
God arose,
Showed me...
Love takes two...
And a lot of prayer
To help me get...
Over you...

Consider The Facts

Consider the Facts

In the beginning, all you saw was me,
You believed,
We were more than a memory
But then you walked away;
Not once but three times you left me,
Standing alone,
I tried waiting for you to agree to disagree,
Tired of being everything you wanted me to be,
Everything you couldn't See,
You just wanted to be Free.....

Run Away, Fly Away,
have your Freedom,
But LET ME BE ME!
Don't play the victim
Hiding behind the system for your lack of
belief…..
Sitting on your supreme throne,
Casting condemnation
Demanding explanations
Without an imagination….
I tried waiting for you to agree to disagree,
Tired of being everything you wanted me to be,
Everything you couldn't See,
You just wanted to be Free…..

Whose to blame
For abomination, discrimination, and bad
reputation of our civilization?
Who Cares about the answers,
But you wanted information
The source of my inspiration,
Without observing what makes me ME…
You wanted FACTS
Kept attacking
Without ever checking
Other Aspects
My heart….
But it all fell through….
With just a VIEW

I tried waiting for you to agree to disagree,
Tired of being everything you wanted me to be,
Everything you couldn't See,
You just wanted to be Free…..

Consider the facts….
What Truly matters…
Was it me?
I'd be inclined to disagree...

Crazy Theory

Had this crazy theory

Turned out it was just a wild notion

With high hopes.

I believed in devotion

I believed in love felt emotion,

But you were just playing the game;

Making false implications of love,

the lies slipping from your lips,

Words gripping with underlining disguise,

Unwilling to compromise,

Making justifications to satisfy

THE FACT that

YOU were just biding time.

Bitching and Whining

Confining our Love

Blindly convincing yourself

I was the one hiding, lying, trying,

to destroy our silver lining

By complaining and crying …

Condemning you to a life of hell

Holding you in a prison cell of standards

For all of man's manners slandered

By the commands of my brainwashed illusions

That there Something Far Greater than you or
I…

I had this Crazy theory….

I Believed in YOU…..

Women Hurt

Women Hurt
Bittered by abandonment
On a massive mission
Collision …
To seek and Conquer
A deeper seeded friendship

Established slowly over a journey
That speaks a language
Far beyond any expression of words
In this World…
It's a Genuine fondness

That understands
Turns the world we observe
Into lessons served
Preserving an emerging
Force of nature…
That has been burned...
Disturbed by
A turning in our Universe...

Women Scorned
Be forewarned;
Ignored and abused
By her accused
Oh Dear Lord ;
Have mercy
On his poor soul
For what she has in Store…

Done wrong to
One too many times…
Where does she fit??..
Where does she belong;
Born so strong …
Armed in a harness of Strength
All she waits for in this war
Is the secret power
To Explore More.

A Single Tear I Cry For you:

A single tear I cry for you,
A tear of a love that has been lost
Before the dawn of the first frost.
A tear of a hope forever gone,
Drawn from a last breath
In death…
A Single tear that
I held dear in my heart,
From the start;
Has torn us apart
Like a master expert;
Without any effort,
A single tear I cry for you.

A single tear I cry for you
At night the light of the moon
Cresting the Sky;
Doesn't even dry my wet tired eyes;
When I realized what we had
Could not withstand the unplanned.
Because now you are nestled in your resting
place
While I digest this protesting;
Our Fate.
We had a blessing

Many lessons that often kept us guessing,
Now I find myself requesting more time
Wrestling with the fact that you're gone.
A single tear I cry for you;
A hope forever I carry,
Has been buried
Because you alone;
Will Always Be….
A part of me.
Even in the times
We spent disagreeing
You didn't have to be perfect;
You had to be you…
That's all that ever mattered to me.
I did not want to change you;
I just wanted a chance to explain
What I had gained
Even when you complained…
And our souls grew faint
I knew that mountains could be moved
Countless times I prayed,
A prayer you…
A single tear I cry for you…
I cry … and cry…
I cry for you…. Nobody but for you.

A single tear I cry for you.
A tear for the days ahead,
The dread of sorrow,

Looming over
My overwhelming hurt of Tomorrow.
A Single Tear I cry for you.
I shed each night I lay down my head
To sleep at night…
Too weak to even speak'
Beneath the surface my breaking heart whimpers
and weeps;
Trying to keep it together
I must go on;
My brain warns its easier said than done;
A single tear I cry.
I cry for you…Nobody but for you.
A lifeless empty shell
Suddenly extinct from existence,
A distant memory fading away
This constant Absence
With a single Tear, I cry through sad red eyes,
A wound grounded to deep
My tears drown me surrounding
Me with the knowledge you are no longer
around…

A Tear with meaning that only I comprehend,
Attentive Well-meaning Friends offer a hand
Trying to understand...
But the brokenness won't mend;
People stare wondering Why…
I pretend not to care;

In the end,
God Sends his Grace...
But the tears I still Cry
I don't want this to be your Goodbye.
I want to hear you call me your Angel;
No matter how painful…
I want to hear the songs
Of your heart
I want a restart
Without you departing
Leaving me alone without you
Guarding me with your subtle charm
And stubborn ways...
I'd do anything to get back those days.
A single Tear.

A single tear of love,
And hate,
One that turns our fate
To dust,
You were my Crutch
When life was passing me by
Taking me for a ride.
A tear that collects your memory
After a century,
Of Developing our identities.
But I still think of You
Till I can no longer stand
But it does not change

The fact you are no longer my man…
A single tear I cry for you.

Who knew,
What I
Would go through?
It has to be untrue
I don't want to believe
There is not a Me and You.
Dreaming Dreams &
Holding onto what we'd pursue…
I had no clue
I am left alone with my thoughts
My stalking madness that you loved to hate
Now brings a slight smile to my face…
In the times my mind takes a dive,
I will use these faults
You pointed out as a source of strength
To keep me strong…
I'll still rely on you for support;
Even though physically
You can no longer take away my misery
I still have that tear
One that will always be engraved
With your name

If My Heart Had Wings

If My Heart Had Wings
I'd know what it's like to Fly
To Ride this world on clouds
High above through the Sky….
If my Heart Had Wings…
I'd find a way to bring you
back to my side…
We could couple hand in hand
Stand against the wind
If My Heart Had Wings
I'd know what it felt like to sing
Never give up
Never give in.
If My Heart Had Wings
I'd bring you back

Would not think twice to react
Or have second thoughts
If My Heart Had Wings
Harps and violins
Would begin
To ring
Reminding me of
All the heavenly things
That brings calming comfort
To a heart that
Stings with
Bitterness
At all the unfairness that life brings
Within my reach as I am clinging
To straws grasping for hope
I wish my Heart had wings
So that I could
See you one last time;
Rewind to our last goodbye
So the tears I would no longer cry…
Finding you back beside me:
Where you belong…
If My Heart Had Wings
I'd fly up to heaven's doors
I'd soar those clear blue skies
Find the Joy I Had Before...
The day I lost you...

The Child's Gone Now Lives a Woman Inside

No longer that young girl who depended upon
you
This little girl grew up, she no longer gives a
damn
She found another man…
That guy ain't you making her life misery...
He's busy loving her,
Not picking a fit bitchin
Better back off
Or it'll cost you
You'll need a stitching..
Wishing you hadn't gone there.
No longer that little girl you once controlled
With that winded hot air
Now she just doesn't care...
Don't give a damn...
She found another man...
Standing by her side
Lovein her for who she is
Now she can't stand you…
Knowing she'll always be his
Bitch…
So kiss this ass as it walks pass
And wish you didn't let go

Because your brain was too
Screwed
Too slow to comprehend she loved you...
But now she's loving someone new
No longer waiting and hoping you'd come
through
She's no longer that child you once trampled
Dampened her spirits
Cramping her style with all the lies
Telling her you cared
But never shared
Any piece of your heart
Just leaving her
Hurt…
Now she has a dude
That's tougher than you…
He has the right sorta passion
Intensity,
He understands
Her like no one knows
Because only he has taken the time to find
What's hiding inside
He looked beneath the surface
Now they have a purpose
They build a future...
She's no longer a child
But a woman
That's learned many lessons
Now she has a destination without you…

The child's gone
She's grew
Now lives a woman inside….
No longer by all the lies…
Tearing her apart

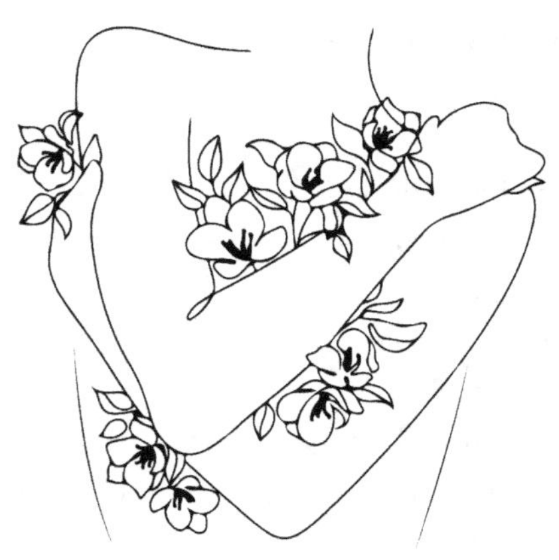

Dirty Little Secrets

Am I no better than you?
With DIRTY LITTLE SECRETS
A closet full of skeletons;
Buried somewhere deep inside,
Waiting to be released
To expose me for who I am…?
DIRTY LITTLE SECRETS from the past
Tearing me apart….
Wanting freedom from the bondage of my heart,
A place to confess my disgrace;
Without feeling ashamed for who I am…
Because those DIRTY LITTLE SECRETS
Keep tearing me alive….
The difference between you and I…

I have found my prayer room
To the one who knows me best.
For the Sinner I am….
The one that doesn't Judge me for being me;
But loves me,
Because I was created to live a legacy…..
Even with every DIRTY LITTLE SECRET.
I take it to the chambers of my heart;
Where I'm confronted by;
Lies in disguise...
Agonizing Secrets jeopardizing;
My salvation
As I rationalize this fraudulent
Character I've become
DIRTY LITTLE SECRETS
Taking them to Jesus
Looking to find completeness
But instead consumed by weakness
From temptations that inflame my shame;
Deceivingly misled
By the voices in my head;
DIRTY LITTLE SECRETS
Keep me hanging by a thread;
Crying wishing I could remove the voices in my
head,
But my God Said;
"For Those Tears, I died…."
DIRTY LITTLE SECRETS

My Prose, My Angel

He wants to fix the broken pieces
Wants to release this mess
Take away all the stress…
Wants to help me find
Some rest
All he wants is to make me happy;
To see me smile
Just for a little while
He's my best friend…
Our hearts bond
They blend
They just connect…
Collecting melodies
Finding a rhythm of its own
He calls me his prose
Our sequence just flows
while my affection seems to grow...
His words seduce my thoughts
Leaving me at a loss…
Melting this fortress;
Removing…
Barriers; closing the distance,
Exposing things no one else knows
He polishes all those
Tiny imperfections that compose

The elements of who I am….
AND
All he wants is to make me happy;
To see me smile
Just for a little while
He's my best friend…
Our hearts bond
They blend
They just connect…
Like written language
He manages
To pull through the
Mangled mess of baggage
Taking advantage
Of the tangled
Challenges of a damaged
Package wrapped up
In this heart of mine
That dangles
Without anchorage
Keeping this anxious soul
Uncontrolled adrift...
Without any direction
Without a guide…
But
With just one look
There he is
By my side ready to provide
A stable

Place to reside…
My prose you arose
As a stranger,
My Angel
Protecting me
From painful changes…
From all of life's dangers

Her House Still Stands IN Praying Hands...

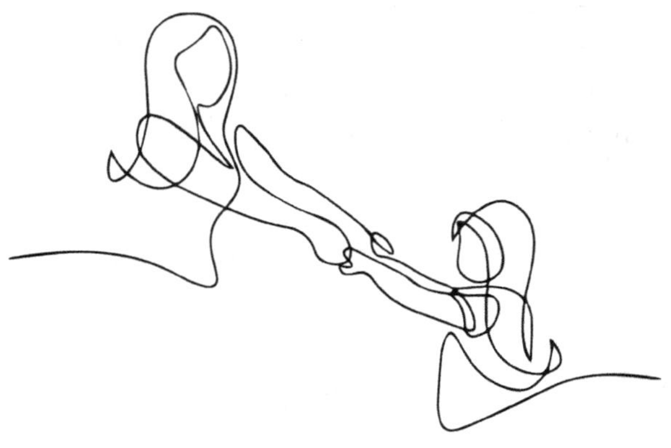

Cracks on the Walls
Scream throughout the halls
Fractures in the crevices
Can be seen...
Nick marks the floors,
From long years of wear and tear,
Broken down by the batter of scattering small
feet...
Scratches appear on the door…
Where...
Scrubby tiny hand prints smear the glass
A gentle reminder life moves along too fast…
In a house that echoes decaying
Waiting to be destroyed,
Stands a mother praying…

Wishing and hoping the foundation remains
firm…
Confidant in the Promises of a much higher
Power
Devouring crowds of cowards
Empowered by an inspiration
Influenced by her secret relationship
A partnership of sacrifice…
Living in a fool's Paradise
Enticed at times by impatient temptations
Of destruction
Ready to erupt corruption in the home she's built
By her personal instruction manual...
Signed in blood
Written with Love…
In a home that threatens to fall apart…
Stands the heart of a mother
Who has been hurt, but forgives
Admits to her own imperfections
She strives to do better
lives to give…
Without Objection
She does not Question...
Mentored by simple direction,
An example of a legacy,
That has lived on forever...
Anchoring her home on the Rock
Nothing blocks the faith she's found
Grounded Within…

Though Cracks are in the archways
Up and down the entry,
It's her friendly sanctuary
A place she finds comfort
A place she calls home…
Her House Still Stands in Praying Hands…

The Lions Gate

The Lion at the Lions Gate
It was more than,
You bargained for...
You spent decades,
Trying to even a score...
I never took to explore...

The Lion at the Lions Gate,
He's the king ...
That decides your fate,
Before it's too late.
All the...
Witchery, gossippin.
Voodoo dolls...
And a little moon magic...
It won't stop the ticking
Of the clock...

The intimidating power,
Of the Lions ROAR,
Can be heard from;
Heavens door...
Restoring justice,
Balancing the universe

All you noticed,
Was that lure
Fame and fortune
Profit is all you could see...

The Lion at the Lions Gate,
Held more importance...
Then you claimed...
Enslaved to misbehave
Repeating a ...
toxic Karmic Cycle

If it came Down to You &
Me

If it came down to you and me
In a ring of a Golden Grand Trine
I'd wish for it to be your time
To shine...
I'd manifest
All that brings you
Joy and happiness
And even though you aren't
With me, I'd pray for your blessings
To fall showering you every day
When life starts to wrestle
With the rest and peace
Of mind.
I'd ask the good Lord
BE kind,
Allow you to find
All the love that your heart desires,
To supply you with an entire radical
Support that justifies an alignment
Of cosmos rebellion...
My wish would be,
My hellion,
Would....live
Well...and...free

If it came down to you and me
In a ring of a Golden Grand Trine
I'd wish for it to be your time
To shine...
I'd manifest
All that brings you
Joy and happiness

Just Another Wish Upon a Star

Just another
Wish upon a star
Just another
Dream so big
Only heaven could
Ful-fill ... ...
Everyday miracles,
Needing the faith
To believe...
No ordinary destiny...
Comes without.....-
Trails... ... tribulation... ...
Abit of... ....sacr-fice... ...
Too... ooo ...
Wait-ing - ex-pect-ing-ly -
For blessings -
From above...
To flow through-
Wrapping me in...
The arms of love...
Just another
Wish upon a star
Just another-
Dream so big

Only heaven could
Ful-fill ... ...
Every day I love... ...
You... ... -even-... ... -more-... ..
My hearts ready
To explore... ...
All that fits perfectly... ...
To this firm found-a-tion.
Your un-con-di-tion-al
Love....
Everyday miracles
Needing the faith
To trust in you
To believe that
Dreams do come true.

FRamed in Fame

I may never get a lyric Framed in Fame,
May never hear one SONG sung on the radio,
But in my heart, I've already reached platinum
To me you're Gold

I may never get to tell you face-to-face,
may never be able to sing you a chord,
But in my heart, you were almost as high
As my Lord…
To me, You were my saving grace…
My comforting place.

Your loving healed me
From being a vengeful Bitch,
A conning snitch just waiting;

To rip apart any man
I couldn't stand….
Your love was Gold
To me….
You STOLE my heart
With One Kiss…

You Sealed OUR Fate
In just ONE date
The love shared,
The up-and-down rollercoaster,
Closer and closer
Shoulder to shoulder
Over and over again…
 Intrigue crippling me;
 Disease…driving me…crazy…
Crownig~me~dizzy~in~a~frizzy…
Manic love affair

What a destined work of Art…
A defining destiny
Written in the stars.
Written in the
Words of
Every poem,
Every song,
In every tragic romance gone,
Every fairy tale story
That didn't have a happy ending

All those years spending many
Times
Living,
Learning,
Forgiving,
Listening…
to the rhythm we shared.
Nothing Compared
With all thats
Been shared…

My song began with you
My song ended with you…
Every line,
Every word,
prepared from a heart
That hurt...
In losing everything
Worth living for…
You were my purest reward
In you I found Gold …
Courage to prepare
Every careful prayer
Despite the scars
That were too scared.
Barely breathing…
You were my reason,
My season,
For Believing….

Judgment of the King

The day the sky went dark
God turned his face
Closed his heart
Watched his son
Pay the price
As he stretched out
His arms
And Bled…
God Wept

The day the sky went dark
Marks that pierced the flesh and covered
A body that suffered

A tortured price paid
In the name of Agape
As a mother watched
With discomfort
Her only son,
Beaten and bleeding,
As the heathen kept
Repeating the heated
Mistreating. ..
Over and over
Swinging their whips and chains
Demanding he begs for his freedom
God Wept
Turned his face,

The day the sky went dark
Jesus laid down his life for
The human race
He brought to them
A sacrifice of love
That will one day Return
From above…
When the Judgment of the King
Takes his wings
On a chariot
Coming forth
To carry his people
From the decaying evil ….

One day the judgment of the King
Will bring
An understanding of all the things
That kept us wandering...
One day On a horse and Chariot
There will be no more sorrow
The sacrifice that carried
My debt :
will come to collect…
Those tears that were cried
Will be dried
The Judgment will reign….

Sleeping On The Job

I had a job for you to do,
I called to you,
You did not hear,
I whispered in your ear,
Again you thought
I was not near.
Sleeping on the Job.

I had a job for you to do,
You never knew,
I sent you a voice,
You made your choice,
You followed others,
Not me.
You had the fruits of my tree,
You had the seed to set
man free,
Sleeping on the job.

I had a job for you to do,
I had to pass you by,
You did not desire
To inspire others
With what you knew,
To be true,
That Jesus paid the debt
That would one day

pay the price for man's sin...
You did not win souls,
You let my light dim.
You lost my shine
Sleeping on the job.
Your joy faded,
I waited...
I had a job for you to do,
I asked you to plant the seeds,
I asked you to water my garden,
To tend the flowers to help them grow,
But you did not sow the seed
Instead, you made way for the weeds,
Of sin and doubt,
My garden did not sprout,
You allowed the soil to dry out,
You did not use the proper tools...
My Word,
You left unheard,
Sleeping on the job.....
I had a job for you to do,
You did not listen,
Now you are
Missing my blessings,
I tested your faith,
You were too late,
Your blessings had
already been replaced.
Sleeping on the job.........

www.ingramcontent.com/pod-product-compliance
Lightning Source LLC
LaVergne TN
LVHW021240200726
843509LV00012B/1549